I'M NOT
THE SAME
AGAIN TODAY

I'M NOT THE SAME AGAIN TODAY

my lessons from a lyrical life

LAINEY OSLIN

EMPOWERED
PRESS

Published in the United States by Empowered Press Publishing LLC, Las Cruces, NM

ISBN 978-1-957430-20-1 (paperback)

ISBN 978-1-957430-21-8 (ebook)

Library of Congress Cataloging-Publication-Data is available.

Library of Congress Control Number: 2024931531

http://theempoweredpress.com

publish@theempoweredpress.com

Cover design: Onur Aksoy

http://onegraphica.com

Layout design: Katie Moody

The Empowered Press can bring authors to your live event. For more information or to book an event please email: publish@theempoweredpress.com.

To Katie and Charlie, for being with me through the worst and the best of it.

And to Ric, for being the reason it was all worth it in the end.

contents

author's note

It happened on a plane.
Dallas to Seattle; just after the world opened back up.
I was a little too overtired, the frozen shoulder I'd been battling was complaining to the rest of my body, my seat felt too small, and the four-hour flight ahead of me felt endless.
I was fussy and in pain but getting ready to tuck in and endure it.

Then the cabin temperature dropped on takeoff to a level far below what was comfortable.
I was suddenly freezing and constricted.
And just like that,
the internal click of the launch sequence began.
The cold caused every feeling I was having to magnify.
The assigning of blame triggered immediately and was generously spread.
Resentment at things like this 'always happening to me'.
Life's ultimate targeting of me for unfairness.
Hating everyone around me for not being cold and uncomfortable too.
Prepared to play martyr to its limits.
A two-year-old melting down in the freezer section of a Safeway.

I waited.
I watched it.
I knew what this was now.

I'd just learned not to let it off its leash anymore.

Much larger and even smaller versions of these emotional hailstorms have littered my lifetime.
It's not that I had it worse than anyone else,
it's that the size of my feelings didn't seem to fit inside,
and would often spill over,

demanding immediate attention and soothing that often wasn't accepted.
What was essential is that my discomfort be known,
and that everyone at least try.

When you live with emotional anxiety,
you learn to cultivate a crew designed to calm you down.

In some ways I'm not nearly as bad as I'm making myself sound.
I have earned my place in the lives of those I love.
I have lived wide and loved deeply,
and given large parts of myself away for the benefit of others.
But I have also been known to corner the market on emotional real estate, leaving no room for anyone else to feel anything.

'Attention: I will be starting at nuclear and will require volunteers to walk me back to reason. You'll easily find me by all the noise and broken dishes,
or deadly silence and passive aggression.
Must be prepared to have all suggestions rejected,
and the right to 'rage-redirect' with you as the target will be reserved.'

A meltdown during quarantine was the last time I let myself learn life the hard way.
The miracle in the aftermath was that I finally saw myself,
through the eyes of those I had caught in the chaos.
I wasn't being understood,
I was being 'managed.'
It was no longer about compassion,
it was about containment.

I was the one being endured.

My life has been blessed with those who love enough about me,
to help carry what I cannot at times.
But when need is determined to be endless,
even the greatest heroes get exhausted.

You gotta be worth the trouble.

The other side of this is that the world needs us.
We are the ones who can plumb the depths of the deepest loves,
and the darkest pains.
We add color and carbonated cacophony,
and often delight our audiences with our full-spectrum
humanness.

The problems arise when the gratitude we feel for our calming
crew,
turns to entitlement.

Simply the cost of our company.

What we supply,
stops being worth the demands that accompany it.
If balance is not restored to the emotional teeter-totter,
eventually people stop doing business with us.

When they turned off the seatbelt sign,
I grabbed a sweatshirt from the overhead,
and gave myself two minutes to lean over to my sister and
release the words of what had just happened.
Sharing the rollercoaster in order to dissipate the energy,
but not asking her to ride,
or to rescue.

And then I read my book.

'This was only a test.'
Another chance to see how I've changed.
To once again fail to die from life's discomforts.

That internal 'click' signals something different now.
It tells me a storm is coming,
and my only job until it passes,
is to shelter in place and watch from the window.

I still feel it sometimes,
but I don't feed it anymore.

Shame keeps tapping my shoulder,
insisting that I'm oversharing too early.
Requesting I include a page of excuses and clear justifications.

But the journey we're about to go on together is going to have a
'how' woven throughout,
and it's my job to include the 'who's.'

All of them.

What you're about to read is part memoir,
part poetry book,
part self-help guide,
and on some pages,
part love letter.
With creativity and the outdoors getting a great deal of credit for
everything.

My now-sacred years spent writing my recovery.
Broken down into blinks.
Snapshots.
A mosaic of memories.

I'm a child in some,
still raising them in others.
Terrified of being alone,
but growing to love nothing more.
Grappling with divorce, addiction, betrayal, and grief at times,
deeply grateful for their gifts at others.
In other words, I'm probably everybody,
so if I seem to give advice,
it's because I needed it.

All of the Me's that I am or have been can be found in the
following pages.

There is no favorite,
and they don't appear in any order of importance.

Any one of them would've been worthy of beginning this book.

I just decided to start with the one who used to block all the exits.

I

My now sacred years spent
writing my recovery.

What is this thing that makes us want to shed all we know and start over by walking away?

pct

During the darkest days of my divorce, I developed a craving to hike the Pacific Crest Trail.

Twenty-four years was gone in a blink, and my answer to it seemed to be a desperate desire to take a very long walk.

From the start, I knew if I did, I'd most likely end up needing to be rescued from the scorching desert, or the snowy Sierra Nevada Mountains.

Risking myself to restart my life was all right, risking others would just be reckless and irresponsible. But oh, how I would weep at my wanting to.

What is this thing that makes us want to shed all we know and start over by walking away? What does it mean when a lifetime of accumulation doesn't leave us with one thing that feels or looks the way we thought it would? And now we can't bear to look at any of it anymore.

For me it was the realization of how simply it can all be dismantled. That each life is simply a house of cards subject to the smallest wind that takes it all down. Taking those we love down with it. The best-laid plans are not its problem. The trail is filled with different versions of this understanding, delivered the hard way.

I've had to learn to take my healing in small doses,
Letting countless smaller trails do the honors,
And walking a little 'away' each day.
While measuring the weight of everything I choose to carry.

Life really does come down to the things you hold in your heart or on your back.
The rest is just distraction and decoration.

I'm learning to rebuild while the weather is good, but I'll be more careful about saying 'forever' again.

I know how wind works now.

Did I have words
before the woods?

i'm not the same again today

I'm not the same again today,
thank God.
Changes come in caked mud,
and counted miles.
In deeper breaths,
and covered trails.
Beauty has crossed my path so often now,
that the entanglement is forever tripping me.
Indoor identity giving way,
to lush evolution.

Did I have words before the woods?
Or did I just move my lips for half my life?

What do you see,
when I say the word 'self?'
Whatever it is,
won't be here tomorrow.

Thank God.

origin story

She sat down at the keyboard to write for ten minutes,
but only because she said she would.

The weather was winning.

Each day was a holding cell,
designed so this new version,
could wait for the original to return.

The goals were small:

One multivitamin,
and ten minutes of writing.
The first, an invitation to health,
and the other, to passion.

So far only indifference has responded.

But she said she would,
and this rain can't possibly last forever.

So she took her multivitamin,
and wrote for ten minutes.

I now feel everything I used to deny myself, due to the imagined judgment of others.

2,000

2,000 steps was what I started with.
I wasn't completely broken,
but it wasn't far from where I was sitting,

or lying.

I caught my reflection in a mirror while stepping into the shower
and had the deep awareness I was going to die without ever truly
living in my body.

This body, that has carried me down the gauntlet hallways of
junior high.
Has been addicted.
Has made me a mother.

Twice.

Has weighed much more, and even a little less.
It's brought me through joy and trauma equally.
Walked me down aisles and up courthouse steps.
Held laughter that strained the seams, and wailing to bring the
walls down.

All under constant scrutiny and whip cracking.
All while I stayed safely locked in the upstairs apartment.
This cathedral, under constant siege.

I didn't answer the image all at once,
but the memory of that moment,
might as well have come equipped with a motor.

I now feel everything I used to deny myself,
due to the imagined judgment of others.
And daily meditation brings the white light inside now.

I come downstairs frequently.

When I forget, the woods remind me.
Of my connection and strength.
My wisdom and wildness.
My delight and my divinity.

The woods gave all of me back,
and it all started with 2,000 steps.

what god does | part 1

Sometimes when God closes a door,

he opens two windows just to make it up to you.

recovery

What if I had started my saving sooner,
instead of waiting for it to all be rubble?
Would the trees have been as green,
or the breath as deep?
Would I have known what I was heading off?

Or is wreckage required for the wake up?

Life unable to return to technicolor,
until all shades of shattered have had their say.

Is it normal to grieve the end of grief?
To know I've reached the looking back,
and now the way forward will be expecting the new me I've
become.

I no longer weep for what's been lost,
I only wish I could recover from it all over again.

do not disturb

Everything that feels wrong in me is usually solved,
by simply letting me be alone.

Five years of deep solo research has come down to a single
sentence.

An awareness that the answer was in the activity all along.

Room around me,
to spread my thoughts,
and then think nothing of them.

Letting the upstairs crowd disperse.

What I do with the time varies,
and doesn't matter.
It's the internal returning that does it.

The welcoming of myself back home.

relentless

I drink my morning coffee from a mug my daughter gave me.
It features an exhausted crab smoking a cigarette with the
caption:

'Life Is Fucking Relentless'

Each day I decide if it's a call to action,
or a white flag of surrender.

Am I a worthy adversary?
Or a willing victim?

We get to choose our ass kicking daily.
We'll be worn thin at the other end regardless.

Don't become resigned to your restlessness.
Ignoring it only makes it expand.

Life's persistence demands your attention.

Be fucking relentless right back.

blue

If I was going to spend that kind of money on a coat, then it
needed to be black or gray to go with everything.

Bright electric blue just didn't seem practical.

Somehow, color is a sign of wealth to me.
People who can afford to buy more than one buy the bright
colors.
It never occurred to me that color might be a sign of health.
A Wizard of Oz option, signaling the return from the black-and-
white days.
An investment in being worth more than one,
even if I'm the only one who knows.

But why should I stop there?

There are now 'blue' places I want to go, simply for their beauty,
'blue' ways I want to spend my day,
'blue' food and books just because,
and most of all,
'blue' time,
filled with an abundance of laughter and very little agenda.

It goes with everything.

I feel empowered.

I also feel invisible.

mind games

I'm of two minds,
as if managing one wasn't hard enough.

My indoctrination runs deep.

'Making myself presentable' has always been paramount.
The preparation of my outsides has always taken priority over
the state of my insides.

Until now.

Packaged me doesn't make daily appearances anymore.

Unwantable me.

I told you,
it runs deep.

An underwire doesn't touch my skin anymore.
Rancid make-up has been thrown out and never replaced.
My most useful hair product has become a rubber band.
And out of a closet full of clothes, I choose the same trail-
friendly uniform each day.

The polished version is mostly on pause,
with dating on the back burner,
and discovery on high.

I feel empowered.

I also feel invisible.

There's gold in this grind,
another layer worth digging for.
How can the greatest criticism,

double as permission?

A woman should never 'let herself go.'
But where exactly are we staying?

How can we seek,
when trying to be sought?
Shouldn't our presentation be secondary,
to our divination?
Life is supposed to be lived in stages,
not on them.

And the second act should have less acting.

Of course, one mind tells me I'm running out of time,
but the other knows I'm finally using it wisely.

So don't be surprised if I don't apologize for my appearance
when you see me.
There will be no excuses for my lack of hair and makeup.
'I'm a mess' won't be leaving my lips.

You see, I used the time to write this poem instead.

Simply because I had a mind to.

recovering

When did morning become easier?

The desire for music,
awareness of color,
laughter let go,
to tumble down stairs.

That has to be a good sign, right?

Flavors returned,
savoring remembered,
a wasted frame awakened.

A wondering about what tomorrow will bring.

'Better' on your lips,
when asked.

ohm

I'd been trying to meditate for two years when it happened.
Wondering at the time if I was already doing it,
but just didn't know.

They were mostly guided,
and I was mostly asleep by the end.

I had to keep trying.
It was my only hope for relief.
The alternative was to be eaten alive by a never-ending story.
Remaining trapped in my own torture chamber.

Then one day I was struck by the first moment of nothing.
A blink between my last thought and the next.
The weighted location of nowhere,

flashed,

and then my thoughts flooded in to fill the space.

But I'd done it.
I'd meditated.

If only for a moment.

Once I knew what to look for,
I began to push at the edges,

Until I could swim.

3:33

Why did you wake me at 3:33?
I waited, but there was nothing further.
Did you have a message and I missed it?
Or did you change your mind?
Either way, thank you for thinking of me.

Maybe that's all it was,
a simple 'Hello.'
I've needed it lately,
but you already knew that.
A quick reminder,
that something much larger,
much deeper,
and more constant,
is always at play,
all around me.

It does make the chop at the surface seem silly,
That is, if it wasn't so terribly scary.

So, thank you for the 3's,

They really help.

There's something so freeing about having everything go wrong.

must see

'I would have died without feeling this,'
has entered my mind countless times since life turned the lights
back on.
It's that much more impactful,
because I'd lost a great deal of interest in living in the years
leading up to it.

Not so much depression,
as profound indifference.

Semantics.

My 50's showed up as 'The Decade After I Was Discarded,'
disguised and delivered as the beginning of 'It's Over,'
'The Looking Forward To' years,
long gone.

I hit the halfway-to-60 mark next month,
and I can finally see for miles.

Now that I've stopped blocking the view.

There's something so freeing about having everything go wrong.
The internal attachment to 'right,'
becomes a relative thing.

Having everyone see you fall and fail,
and then follow up by not letting it kill you,
creates that thing we spend our lives searching for:

Immunity to their opinion in the first place.

And finding out some kinds of love are fragile,
somehow lets you finally feel it when it's forged for you alone.

Forgiveness creeps in when you weren't even trying,
and the need to strike back is released.

Simply put, there's just more room.

I'm glad I didn't let go,
and I'm grateful to those who held my tether.

I would never have wanted to miss this.

do over

'If you could relive one day in your life, which would it be?''

We play along.
An exercise in seeking a first-time feeling.
The origin of the echo.

A dopamine do-over.

As for me,
I would go back to my most broken day.
My 'if I could' fantasy,
would take me back to when I couldn't.

I simply want my saving back.

keeping count

Bitter.
The only word I refuse to let touch my name again in this
lifetime.

No small feat at times.

It looks like a pinched face and crossed arms,
and no one wants to talk to that at a party.

Or live with that in a body.

It weighs too much anyway,
since 'Victim' always insists on coming along.

Make that two words.

medicine

Laughter.
The first thing you lose when life goes dark.
You won't even realize how long it's been gone,
until one day, spring dawns in the darkness,
and some random absurdity pushes through the dirt,
giving birth to that which can't be stopped until tears run.

The complete clearing of a clogged system.
Carbonated healing rising from what felt hopeless.

'I don't remember the last time I laughed like that!'
is said once words are possible.

And just like that,

you're going to live.

I always leave a light on,
in case I lose myself again.

moving day

I've finally moved into myself,
after a lifetime of labeled boxes.
Things are finally arranged just so,
and designed to suit only me.
My blueprint is beautiful.

Knowledge and wisdom are featured out front where no one can
miss them.
They distract from the leftover sadness and uncertainty I haven't
put into storage yet.
Each emotion is neatly organized in their own order so as to be
easily accessible:

Love has claimed the largest space and tends to spread out, but
no one complains.
Joy bubbles up from the basement to say hello at least once
a day,
and generally finds worry, sadness, and uncertainty ganging up
again and making a mess in the attic.
Hope doesn't mind staying on the shelf until she's needed,
which is more and more often.
Happiness has her own room but always leaves the door open.
Fear lives out back and sometimes wakes me up at night;
but we're working on that.

My rage is always right where I left it,
and it's too big to move, so I'm waiting until I have help.

I decorate with my dreams,
which are proudly displayed on the walls,
and music accompanies everything.
Inside jokes abound as laughter serves as the diffuser to keep the
air fresh.
I still have a junk drawer that serves as a catch-all for my
fleeting thoughts and partial memories,

but make no mistake,
I'm always down for a dump run.

I'm liberal with the Do Not Disturb sign, so if you're invited in,
then you know you're welcome.
Very few stay the night though.
It's not that I don't want connection,
it's that I now know what it really looks and feels like,
and I won't sacrifice sleep for a substitute.

I maintain my garden for myself,
not the neighbors.

And I always leave a light on,
in case I lose myself again.

II

I'm a child in some.

Still raising them in others.

Try a new trail
every once in a while,
you never know what you'll find.

pussy willow

A slight turn on the trail, and suddenly they were everywhere.
Tiny white dots, peppering the trees.
Fur coats about to burst.
Nature's extravagance on display.

My mom would keep branches in a vase in her bathroom.

I would pet them while watching her get ready,
captivated by both of their beauty.
Snapping a few off for secret soothing later.

My mom in my pocket.

They will always be Pine Lake to me.
Gloria Steinem and Ms. Magazine.
Sex education from Cosmopolitan.
Shalamar and cigarettes.
Neil Diamond and Diana Ross.
Truth or Dare and childhood fears.
Kick the can until we hear the whistle.
Nixon and new stepdads.
Homemade Halloween.
Skipped school, cereal box prizes and,

hours and hours alone in the woods and on the water,
where all of this began.

Try a new trail every once in a while,
you never know what you'll find.

Yesterday I found my childhood.

I hung on his every word.
If he'd lived I may never have
found my own.

dad

He was gone before my prefrontal cortex was fully developed.
I quite literally didn't have the capacity to understand what I was
losing.
It may have been a small mercy at the time.

Each major event in my life since,
has marked his absence.

So has every Father's Day.

I kept waiting for one of his dimes before my daughter's
wedding.
A magically appearing reminder from the other side,
a playful tap on the shoulder.
I wanted to offer it to her and say,
'Grandpa Charlie wouldn't have missed this for the world.'

No harm in rehearsing it.

My son is his namesake.
He gets dimes too.
I found him crying one night, long after lights out.
A seven-year old's heart.
'Where is Grandpa Charlie buried?'
I told him of the ashes and plaque marking the spot.
'Can we go see him?'
The gutting of a child grieving what he didn't get.

I hung on his every word.
If he'd lived I may never have found my own.

It's not something I get to know yet.

But I've done the job of those left behind.
I've kept him fully human and fully here,

through the stories from before.

He was wise and flawed,
funny and complex,
a romantic and a writer,
and missed beyond measure.

It's okay for it to hurt forever.

Weaponized words turn on their maker more often than not.

white flag

I was the youngest of three,
and the one who would never

Shut up!

The last word would be mine,
even if it had to be whispered while walking away.
Earning me more than one punch in the back,
or getting me locked out of the house entirely.

Words made up for my age disadvantage.
They made me feel more powerful,
on the much 'less-than' days.
But absolute power does just what they say,

and weaponized words turn on their maker more often than not.

'There's no talking to you.
You have all the exits blocked.'

I wore it like a badge of honor.

But as the years passed,
what had always felt good flying out,
began to land on locked doors.
And others walking away,
often got mistaken for 'winning.'

Until learning the hard way happened once too often.

I live now, in the pauses,
and pulled punches.
My launch sequence has time built in for review,
and the mission often gets scrubbed.
Leaving the last word up for adoption.

Nothing can grow on scorched earth.

Watch your mouth.
The ones left standing,

often stand alone.

dirt roads

A dirt road covered in potholes and puddles.
Driven like a minefield,
cranking and barely crawling,
every car joint complaining.

We would fill them with gravel,
patching the craters.
The illusion of a solution.
A little less 'country,'
a little higher 'class.'

But only for a minute.

I went back to see this childhood home,
and drove easily down the now paved road.
A different world lives down here now,
with polished words like 'neighborhood' and 'community.'

Why weren't we worth the asphalt?

How do we live out of a dirt-road life?

I'm done doing patchwork.

Sometimes the hard lessons demand to be learned that way.

warning tide

I watched the waves swamp my boy's hiking boots at Second Beach in La Push. He'd sat down to rest on a rock he thought was out of reach of the tide. As I watched it unfold, I wondered if he was aware. If he would pull his feet up in time.
He was.
He just miscalculated,
and he didn't.
But it wasn't a painful lesson to learn,

he knew I had extra socks.

We spend so much of our time trying to help our kids avoid incoming waves.
Often throwing ourselves in the way of the water,
only to have them get wet anyway.

Standing by when we know what's coming is as painful as any torture created.

Anne Lamott once wrote of weeping over her newborn because she knew he'd have to go to junior high school one day.

The pain starts early.

Looking back from my own tsunamis,
I know that a shouted warning wouldn't have changed the outcome.

Sometimes the hard lessons demand to be learned that way.

There's no saving our children from this.

And there's no way of knowing if we've miscalculated.
If we should have stepped in and saved them.

So we take it on a wave-by-wave basis,

and we bring extra socks.

Whatever it is,
we have to feel it while it's fresh,
and then again, once the looking
back comes along.

wild

My daughter annotated the margins of the novel *Wild*,
and gave it to me.

I could barely stand to look at it.

I'm already grieving that I'll never again,
see it for the first time.
A day will come,
when I'm on the last page.

A holy book.

Highlighted passages,
comparisons and observations.
Four years of life squeezed into every blank space.
All of the drives,
hikes,
woods and waves.
All of the grief and growth.
The wonder.
And what it all meant to her.

I wish I had more tears to give it.

The reliving will come rushing back,
page by page.
And I will savor my gutting,
one word at a time,
one trail at a time.

Whatever it is,
we have to feel it while it's fresh,
and then again,
once the looking back comes along.

I'm not afraid to revel in my recovery,
it may very well have been the best part.

what god does | part 2

Sometimes God disguises doors as windows,

and then waits around to see the look on your face when you realize it.

what about the children?

WARNING: It will always be hard.

That's why you're relieved when the subject is changed.

The saying out loud.
The circling back,
to check our healing.

Once life has cooled, we crave moving on.
Why open wounds,
when pretending 'fine' feels natural now?

But this is where the good part lives,
if you can survive the guilt,
and avoid the need to explain.

The floor is theirs now.

What you don't know,
simply awaits their words.

Your children have observed the worst.
The careful illusion of 'Parent' cracked wide.

What did they find there?

You can survive the answer.

custody agreements

Parenting versus partnership.
The post-divorce conundrum,
especially with older children.

Before it all, there was no question,
but the aftermath forces new framing.

We want to show our hand on the rudder.
To prove we've 'got this' and all will be righted,
while standing in a trash dump of wrong.
Credibility in shreds.

How can I possibly know what's going on in their lives,
when I didn't even know what was going on in my marriage?

There is a delicate dance here, in rooms filled with elephants,
grief,
and guilt.
As well as powerless words like, 'Because I said so.'

When do you give a child enough power to participate in their
own rescue?
When do you tighten your grip?
Whatever you decide,
you will be blamed.

Credit only comes after you've climbed out.

Trust that there is still groundwork left from the good years,
and stop leading from what you lack.

Your children will forgive your mistakes,
as long as you were there making them.

ransom demands

Trauma is a hostage taker.
It uses our children as human shields,
knowing we'll never call its bluff,
as long as it's got them by the neck.

I'm in a standoff.

When is a push needed?
What's the final straw?
Red or blue wire?

The perception of a child's pain,
as seen through the broken filter of a mother's guilt.

Some of the best parenting,
is the nothing you do while they twist.

Letting them struggle with a new wound,
may provide the clues to an old one.
Rescue too soon,
and burden them with both.

Be the witness while they suffer,
and the wisdom when it's over.

Trust them to withstand a higher expectation.

And know that while trauma may take them to a second location,
you don't always have to be in the car.

outside the lines

My boy gave himself another tattoo.
Writing his insides down on any usable surface.
Creating his own captions.

I once would have minded.

Does a good mother get mad?
Or does a good mother just act mad,
to avoid the judgment of other mothers?

Or because her own mother did?

I can no longer find it in me,
to suppress what he finds in him.

The undoing of the indoctrination has begun.

For both of us.

*Past stories can be put aside
when it matters,
and room can be made
for new chapters.*

she will

We're planning a wedding here.
Three months to put together a June ceremony,
from invitation to aisle walk.

Our own personal mountain.

There are two timelines for me.
One is the blink that brought my daughter from baby to bride.
And the other is every exquisite and painful step that made our
montage.

Leaps forward trigger the looking back.

Each person who was in the room when she was born,
will be there watching,
just from different sides of the aisle now.

A reminder that we all still agree on one thing.

I will always leave room for the 'How did we get here?',
and then I'll switch timelines again.

It's possible.
Past stories can be put aside when it matters,
and room can be made for new chapters.

Time marches on.

My daughter will be taking the walk that proves it.

I know I'll be grateful that grace made the guest list.

mellow

'Mellowing with age,'
may very well be my new favorite activity.
A side effect of time worth getting excited about,
if it were worth the extra trouble of doing so.

I only notice it due to the nothing that happens,
in the space where wildfires used to burn down villages each
time life began to ad lib.

Acceptance finally moving into where I thought it lived all
along.

My daughter is getting married this weekend,
and there are hot spots everywhere, threatening to ignite into
actual problems.
Unseen roadblocks, last minute omissions, and Covid for all the
most important players.

This is the stuff.
Circumstances that would make me pack a bag,
and take up residence in the top two inches of my throat.
Doing my best to embody the word NO.

What's showing up instead looks a little more like reason,
humor, and maybe some polite indifference.
I've seen life burn down before,

this isn't it.

We will continue to dot and cross details,
a rehearsal will ensure it all goes as planned,
the music will start,
the people will stand,
and something unexpected will happen.
A room full of feelings,

mixed with different personalities,
almost guarantees it.

But on this day next week,
when reflecting on the love and laughter,
I know I'll be grateful that grace made the guest list.

It hasn't missed an event yet.

And if someone goes sideways,
well, there's grace in that too.
Because due to my new personality trait,

I know it won't be me.

Words mixed together with tears and laughter.

she did

It rained off and on,
but it didn't matter.
It simply washed the world clean for their own personal use.

She wanted me near her from the start of the day,
and kept claiming 'bride's rights' to keep me close.
Her gift of a necklace,
engraved with a rose.

The only middle name I would agree to,
hasn't left my neck since.

The girls she grew up with led the way,
and I met her dad's eye halfway up,

bringing what we did right on his arm.

Words mixed together with tears and laughter.
Then a kiss locked it all into place.

I sat in the front,
leaning into the one I'll be having my own words with soon.

If there were any hard feelings,
we all left them at home.
For a day, we weren't damage from a difficult divorce,
we were the handful of people who were in the room when she
was born.

All of us, stunned by the trick time can do.

Her dance with her father,
was my own personal highlight.
I called out 'Do kicky leg!,'
which launched them unscripted,

into her childhood.
Transporting us all back to another time,
and a living room full of love and laughter.

She cried at the end,
'Was it really okay?'
A child's hope and held breath,
about all that's been out of her hands.

I gave her the truth as a wedding gift.

Congratulations, Peach.

What if the other version had played out instead?

family photo

There's an image on a table at the end of my bed.
Me with both of my children.
I'm looking down at my little blonde ditto,
with the other still safe and growing on the inside.

It lives directly in my eyeline when I'm writing.
All I have to do is look up.

I was walking through these last years of my work,
trying to organize my blinks,
into what would one day be this book,
when I caught myself wondering:
What if the other version had played out instead?

Where three remained four,
and illusion stood in for love.

And everyone mostly remained inside.

Would they have witnessed my withering?
Seen me as a cautionary tale?
Would I have become 'what not to do?'

My children have traded off riding shotgun for this five-year
hero's journey.
They saw the denial,
but also the determination.
They've seen the tripping,
and they've witnessed the retread.

I can only give them what actually happened,
and show them no shame for what I did about it.

I'm glad I looked up.

III

Grappling with divorce, addiction, betrayal and grief at times.

we think there's something going on

'He would never' was how I opened every answer.
There was no question in my conviction.
In fact, the words left my lips so frequently, at times I may have
said them accidentally.

With no idea that I was talking in my sleep every time.

I'd even blur them together so as to leave no spaces for
reflection.
Hewouldneverhewouldneverhewouldnever.
It became a kind of mantra.
A weighted blanket of words meant to suffocate my instincts.

A chanting child with covered ears.

At times I would add to either end of it.
Making my denial deeper or at least more decorative.

But he would never.

Wait, he would never.

He would never **do that.**

He would never **be able to live with himself**.

Spoken as a spell that would transform them into solid form,
and fit them neatly into my pocket.

A worry stone against the truth.

He

Would

Never

Do

That

Four out of the five words were right.

It will all be worth it,
because I will never again choose
anyone who isn't.

alone

I'm going to be alone.

The size of this sentence cannot be overstated.
In a life that has been spent married and raising children,
it comes just after your slate is erased.

'I am his wife'
'I am their mother'
'I am wanted'
'I am needed'
'I am valued'

Now I'm not.

It's a monster.

And your fear of it will drive you into a new relationship long
before you've had a chance to determine who you actually are
now that new captions are in order.

Friends know it, otherwise they wouldn't be reassuring you on a
loop that, 'Someone is going to snatch you up.'

And believe me,
I've tried.
I've even met a couple of 'box checkers' who I really did try and
settle into.
But resistance keeps winning.
Something keeps pulling me away.

I get to be alone.

I definitely want something from someone,
someday,
but not yet.

And I'm not going to waste this time pretending I'm not
reveling.

Because I will miss it when it's gone.

One day snoring will wake me again,
or I'll shave my legs before bed,
just in case.
I'll compromise on the heat or AC,
or leave the lights off at 2 a.m.,
even though my writing needs me.
I'll say, 'I don't know, what do you want?,'
when it comes to eating,
and I'll bite my tongue when it comes to driving.

And if I ever have suspicions,
then I will once again have my independence.

It will all be worth it,
because I will never again choose anyone who isn't.

That is, once I decide to start choosing.

There's still a little fear.
Like once I'm finally ready,
my time will be up.
My 'best if used by' date long since passed.

Used by.

Old conditioning has a vice grip.

For now, I starfish sleep in the same bed I eat cookies in,
while I long to long for someone to be there,
but don't just yet.
And I'll keep digging deeper into the partner I want to be,
eventually.

And once I meet him,
he won't mind leaving me alone.

You're only prolonging your pain.

life and death

While in labor with my son,
my doctor declined to boost my epidural.
The blooming, unexpected size of the pain,
had me powerless, terrified, and angry.

I refused to push.

The doctor and I were in a standoff.
The ultimate example of trying to control Life.

It was not a battle I won that day.

My son was born,
and I moved on to my next resistance.

Divorce is often compared to death.
And while that's true, and worthy of the volumes written on it,
it's the labor of birthing a new life that brought me back to that
day in the delivery room.

Powerless, terrified, angry.

And while others may take shortcuts,
and preorder their next chapter,
in an effort to avoid the pain of transition,
the rest of us are forced to gut it out.
Biting down on our grief till our teeth crack.

'You're only prolonging your pain.'

It was true when my doctor said it that day,
and has remained so.
Regardless of my refusal to accept.

I think that's what sent me outside.
To see life after death on a loop.
Putting myself in front of the proof,
that I am perennial.

And something more alive may be coming.

baited

Wait.

Whatever you do, don't send it.

There's more you could tell,

but don't say it.

The trap designed to draw you back in,

should lie empty at your feet.

Your life is too big for this now.

Walk away.

At some point
it has to stop being about them.

ambiguous

I finally have a name for it.
Ambiguous loss.
When 'closure' is for the lucky ones.
When we're forced to live on without ever really knowing.

Loss, as a life sentence.

The end of my twenty-four-year marriage was an elaborate game
of Red Light, Green Light.
Lots of activity going on when my back was turned,
followed by, 'Nothing to see here,' when it wasn't.
I never got the conversation for clarity,
only a smattering of details about the other life.
We never even sat down with our kids together.
Just resistance and distance.
Ghosted on a grand scale.

Eighty percent of what happened will probably always be a
secret to me,
but another drop of the deception was delivered to my door
one day,
and got me wondering if the second half of my life was going to
be spent,
figuring out which parts of the first half weren't a lie.

At times it's a blessing,
to never know when or how many.
To protect what was good,
and hope that some of it actually was.
Desperate to hold onto the light in those we have loved.

The curse is in the story starting again,
each time a new detail is revealed.
It's normal for the mind to seek sense,
when there is none,

so we pick the wound and make it fresh.

Lather, rinse, repeat.

It's not really all that unusual.
It's often not even intentionally evil.
It's an inability to be accountable.
An unwillingness to address.
Simply leaving the field midgame after skirting the rules.

There is comfort and pain in how common it all is.
The comfort is the community you gain,
with amazing company and enduring compassion.
The pain is in being a cliche,
an old story,
told too often.

At some point it has to stop being about them.
What has happened isn't nearly as important,
as what's going to.
The need to play in the maze will lessen,
and the new story you're writing will simply be more interesting.

You may even find yourself leaving the field too.

It just takes longer when you don't have all of the pieces.

reruns

I got trapped in the retelling the other day with all the old
players:
Pounding heart.
Pressed throat.
Damp palms.

Wearing the story one more time.
Creating deeper grooves of verbal tread.
Living in what leveled me,
as if the implosion had only just happened.

We know every word of how we were wounded.

It's the recovery that should be on repeat.

Time will do
what she's always done.

labor

Divorce is the delivery room where the version of you that you'll never meet is born.
Where the you, who will live on in the minds of the other side, takes its first breath of rewritten history.

Every action from this day forward will be assigned an intention in the shape of their story,
Along with the details of why you deserved it.

You'll fight this phantom for years,
Doing your best to correct the record, only to find your efforts have been assigned an alternate agenda.

This will happen even over the most innocent of exchanges.

Yes, it will feel like a house of mirrors,
No, It doesn't matter how many years they knew the original.
(The comparison to grieving a death comes from this part.)

But time will do what she's always done,
By helping the debris and rubble find their final resting places,
She may even donate some of herself to you,
so you can finally hear yourself think.

And it's in those quiet moments that you'll begin to hear the voice of another version born that day.
As small and weak as she was, I'm not surprised you didn't see her.
Sitting alone, with the seeds of your second act tucked safely inside.

She's the one you've been raising while the other one took all the attention,
the one whose similarities end at appearance.

The you who is more you than any you you've ever been,
and she can no longer be bothered to keep track of impostors.

what god does | part 3

And sometimes God closes both,

because you were in the wrong house.

*You leave with what you learned
and who you loved.*

my name is

In the movie *An Unfinished Life*, Robert Redford says, 'Living
with an addict is like living with someone who has C-4 strapped
to their chest. You never know when it's going to go off again.'
I have no point,
I just thought you should know.

My brain has been trying to kill me since I was nineteen.
You can't miss it.
It's the one tapping its foot and checking its watch.
Any day now.

But not today.

A girlfriend came to me for parenting advice.
It's simple:
'Whatever you decide, you will be blamed.'

Our lives are a series of stacked choices.
Most of them we never made.
Make sure the mess you're making,
is your own.

I can give you miles of trail,
but I would prefer to keep my twelve steps to myself.

I miss montages.
The recap of the good parts that remind us it wasn't so bad.
What should we watch,
now that humankind is humancruel?

Addiction feeds on guilt and shame.
Consider this burying the lead.

Gaslight is not a lie,
it's a kingdom of lies,
designed to make your whole life a lie.
The trust you must regain,
is with yourself.

That's two.

I tell everyone to go outside in here,
but find them all in my way out there.
A hidden hypocrite.
Writing it is one thing,
actual dealing is dicey.

I'm a strong believer in,
'one ray at a time,'
taking the sun in small doses,
so darkness doesn't see it coming.
I regret the things I could not change,
but only in secret.
It's called 'anonymous' for a reason.

Do your addiction and subtraction,
and live to surrender daily.
You leave with what you learned and who you loved.
And hopefully a little serenity.

Hi, my name is Lainey.

today at a time

Addiction loves the word tomorrow,
as it rarely has to face it.
Counting on the too muchness of life,
to do the work of creating a perpetual today.

I speak from years of medicating to manage.

Lured into letting it take over my mouse,
while compulsion corrupted all my files.
The promise of the perfect amount of okay,
or at least the endurance of the mundane.

I come as a cautionary tale.

Stop trying to drink the ocean,
the waves will always win.
If you don't believe me,
just ask yesterday.

hot stoves

There are betrayals that are barely endurable.
Intolerable resentments that threaten to swamp us,
until the only relief is to set the feelings on fire,
and label them 'hatred.'

A highly combustible substance,
that almost always detonates at the source.
Consuming its creator.
I tried to hold it,
and couldn't get an ounce over emaciated for three years.

Literally eaten alive.

Fooled into believing my vigilant rage,
was the only thing keeping others accountable.
But finding there was nowhere to go,
with the feelings someone else deserved.

This is where bitter is born.

And that corrosion was where the line was drawn.

Getting loose hasn't been easy,
and trips back have been sporadic.
But I catch the flood quickly now,
and remember why I left in the first place.

I've had to feel the deepest sadness,
while not dying from it,
and contemplate my own unclean hands.

Accountability isn't just for others.

Let go of, 'Who do you think you are?',
in favor of, 'Who do I want to be?'

dam it

I created dams during the family building years.
Storing my power,
and pooling my resources,
for the greater good.
Watering my loved ones,
and lighting the way.

But I stayed in place,
long after the landscape had changed.
Keeping myself backed up.
Dreading the deluge.

But what if I'm the watershed I've been waiting for?

And my world is simply waiting to be washed clean?

scar tissue

I once had to stay off my knee while it healed,
but I waited too long,
and atrophy set in.

Years of recovery followed.

The same thing happened with my heart.
A comfortable crust formed,
time sealed all wounds,

and well, you know the rest.

masterpiece

We are sculpted by our grief,

seeking meaning as a salve,
and words that will solve,
holding the ocean in empty hands.

Suffering one drop at a time.

Made beautiful as a byproduct.

IV

So if I seem to give advice,
it's because I needed it.

excuse me

Can I borrow you for a second?
You can even choose which one I take.
It can be hearing your baby padding down the hallway,
or the moment you smell the coffee.
But maybe we've started too early.
How about the wave when you're let into traffic?
Or the inside joke at work?
Your own reflection?
What about that song?
Or that first bite?

Was that hope you just felt?
I'll take that second first.

I'm happy to wait until you find something worth noticing.
Flowers are a good go-to,
but maybe too obvious.
A sudden scent that floods your memory,
with long ago comforts.
Or the dime at your feet.
Maybe the seagull in an updraft,
or the hand on your lower back.
All are worthy candidates.
All are capable of pulling you back,
to Now,
to Notice,
you're here.

It'll only take a second.

What you'll learn and
who you'll love,
await your decision.

decisions, decisions

Life unfolds from this moment forward,
and yours is the hand on the rudder.

Launch pads and landing strips,
litter the landscape,
along with yokes to be pushed or pulled.

Will you stay because 'family' is bigger than '*couple?*'
Or go, because '*tried*' and '*tired*,'
really just depends on where you put the '*I.*'

Buy or rent?

Will you wait out what's left?
Or wring out last drops?
Heal the wound?
Or declare the scar good enough?

Homemade or store bought?

Will you chase down their lies till they eat you alive?
Or let them land in the sand,
to wait for the tide?

React or respond?

Will you quit from depletion,
or work to completion?
Let obligation lead?
Or self-preservation?

Work or school?

Will you know that there's *More*,
but take *Less* and say thank you?
Nurture your talent?
Or file it away under '*Someday?*'

Heads or Tails?

Will '*just for today*' get you tomorrow?
Or will step 12 turn to 1 in a blink and a drink?

Accept or change?

Will you let your joy hang,
between a lane change and lost keys?
Or will yesterday's lessons,
return today for a do-over?

Stand up or sit down?

Will you call on your knowing,
or let doubt demand silence?
Let your words affect change,
or file it away under '*too risky*'?

Speak or be silent?

This is not left to chance,
it's all left to choice.
Are you all in?
Or do you give in?

What you'll learn and who you'll love,
await your decision.

what god does | part 4

Sometimes God closes a door and then opens it again,
just to remind you that even God has second thoughts.

i wish

The air is filled with the ungranted,
and the ground is covered in their afterthoughts.
Still we return to the hope of the deepest breath,
and launch our lives skyward again,
and again.

Hoping this time the wind will whisper in our favor.

a new day

Always hold your breath before the sun rises.
Repetition does not imply guarantee.
Your imagined entitlement to light holds no weight here.
Warmth is not your birthright.

Your rise signals another's setting.
Their darkness may poison your dawn,
with fear the night will never end.
So always hold your breath.

reflect

This is where you held the stretch.

The ground on which you were proven.

It's cool to the touch now,
from the 'after' whose feet you sit at.
Wisdom is ripe for your picking.

The losing of your balance,
becomes the using it here.

But never mistake reflecting,
for reflection.
That is how 'stuck' gets installed.

You may always be of your pain,
but you've long since stopped being in it.
The difference between the two,
will determine for how long.

Look back enough to learn,
but not enough to live there.

you're open

Send one signal today.

Go through the motions.
Move your lips to the music.
Hope they won't hit it to you,
but stand in the outfield anyway.

Just one sign,
to let the Universe know you're still in the game.
Do the least you can do,

and watch it work anyway.

crowds

In a room of a thousand,
only one truly wants to be there.
The rest of us are just hoping,
it'll be contagious.

Longing for it to feel,
like everyone else's face looks.
Forcing a round life,
into a square room.

There's a reason you're bursting at the seams.

You don't want it,
you just wish you did.
And believe it or not,
you can knit most of a life together doing that.

But not all.

Internal infidelity means at least one of your selves will
eventually be caught.

In a room of a thousand,
look for the exit.

You don't like crowds anyway.

on being balanced

Be ready.
The healing of life,
will bring massive new growth.
You might even like the overcrowding,

at first

but then you'll name this new development 'problems,'
and set to work solving.
Replacing all the old wishes with new ones.
Seeking 'centered' all over again.

Just like last time.

I've had to dig for new definitions, and have gone to deep dark places for my lessons.

humbled

The humbling comes for us all.

No matter how grand we've grown,
or how many seasons we've seen,
life breaks us all in half at some point and files down our edges,

leaving only our weakness on display.

Our family falls apart.
We're removed from a career that defined us.
We launch ourselves at a lofty goal,
and fall short.
We see a stranger in the mirror as our body betrays us.

Those we love leave us behind.

Any one of these can leave us stripped and exposed,
as people pass by,
and talk behind their hands of 'what used to be.'
Any one of these,
can install a shame deep enough to create a new identity.
And every one of these can shake our very foundation,

leaving rubble as our only remaining resource.

I've sampled from the entire menu,
and endured the chipping away of my absolutes.
I've lived deep in my losses and been crushed under previous
convictions.
I've had to dig for new definitions,
and have gone to deep dark places for my lessons.

And I've learned,
that all the way down at the bottom,

past the denial and under the devastation,
behind the defenses and the broken fortresses,
lies a strange kind of freedom we pray we'll never be faced with:

The place when nothing left to lose,
leads to nowhere to go but up.

single

How it happened doesn't matter,
and the blur makes it all bleed together anyway.
The important thing is,
you're finally alone.

You were never that house,
or the settled-on paint color.
Your story is not framed on the mantle,
or told at the PTA meeting.

You aren't that he's gone,
you're not that you begged.

You were never that sweater.

Or the chair at your book club.

But you are where they were born,
and you're everything you've learned.
And all of it fits perfectly in your new somewhere else.

You are not the goodbye,
but you can be the take care,
to let healing remind you it's waiting.

You must name this separate time 'sacred.'
Soon enough,
alone will be over again.

marooned

Make your time on the shore matter.
When you're washed up, don't waste it.
You may be a bit blue, and worn from erosion,
but your edges are smoother,
and you've created new coastline.

There will be time for solid ground later.
Where you'll plant your feet,
and raise your fist,
daring the tide to come get you again.

But this is the time for breath catching,
and stock taking.
You've survived the spitting out,
and you're safe where you are sitting now.

Your shipwreck demands your reflection.

weathered

Life's weathering is much like soil erosion.
Both eventually expose everything.
Painful failures demanding reflection,
gradually revealed,

defying orders to stay underground.

But all that time in the dark,
may have left you in possession of a masterpiece.

Broken parts,
somehow beautiful when bundled.

A bouquet wrapped and ready to be given away.

These are the years meant for teaching.
The point of all your pain.
The part that makes the chipping away,
somehow worth it.

Your shame says I'm a liar,
but it always did have a limited vocabulary.
You would too if your only job was to keep the lights off.

'You' means every part of you,
from roots to wings.
Polish all your hidden places,
you're going on display.

the last five years

Remember when the days were predictable?
We could move from one end to the other,
with little memory of how we got there.
Life on autopilot.
A time when we would challenge ourselves to 'Be here now,'
So we wouldn't miss the good stuff.

Now we live lives of repetitive smelling salts and slaps to the face,
that often leave us punchy and unsteady on our feet.
And just as 'predictable' threatens to make an appearance,
a random rug yank turns us all back into babies with an overactive startle reflex.

The result of all this involuntary attendance,
is that we're definitely 'Here now,'
we'd just like to politely decline.

We long for the good old days that barely had wrinkles before they were gone.

Escaping to how it used to be,
has now become the vacation of a lifetime.
An extracurricular evacuation,
where we can live in our old illusions,
and imagine alternate outcomes.

Is this what it took to pay attention?

All I know is,
the good stuff rarely gets missed anymore.

locked in

It was never supposed to be a prison.
Each piece of life planned and placed so carefully,
until, over time, it simply began to block the sun.

It would be so easy to break free,
but it's safe here,

and at least you have pretty things to look at.

healthy

When we're stuck in what's good for us,
or at least we're trying to be.
They check every box,
save the nameless one.
The illusive 'I just knew,'

stands empty.

We are all masters of self-deception.
Convincing an illusion to fit.
With better than nothing,
taking top honors.

Forcing a 'should'.

Another boat we've all been in,
while desperately bailing water.
Hoping it will break in,
while only wanting to break free.

Another example of life looking the way it doesn't feel.

Guilt is never a worthy guide,
and grief can only delay you so long.

The time you're taking,

belongs to someone else too.

starving

Junk food connections.
People as snacks.
Simply because we need something to do,
while watching the show.

A malnourished life of the top layers.
Maybe sharing the details of a day,
or what we saw online.

Easy enough to cancel if bed sounds better.

Perhaps a crisis is needed.
A moment of something real and revealing.
A pin on a map:
'This is where I saw you last.'

But who wants to chance the nothing that's possible?
Or worse, the too much that now has to be managed?

So we wait for the bell that says, 'Here is what's missing!'
while filling ourselves with place holders.

All the time wondering:
What if we'd just saved our appetite?

stay in

Best to stay in.

The known is here,
and the light doesn't sting your eyes.

Life may be broken down,
but at least everything is right where you left it.

Why chance the wind without a guarantee?
Sure, lift is possible,
but drag is just as likely,
and gambling is how you got here in the first place.

Who knew lonely could be a location?

Life's overlook.

The time for living is later.

Best to stay in.

macro

You're too close.

I've earned this.

Your blinders have blocked all insight.

Don't distract me.

The boundaries have been blurred.

You don't understand.

There's more to life than outcome.

I've worked too hard to stop.

The love is getting lost.

How dare you.

You're too close.

unspoken

Don't say it.
Let the outrage ricochet off your ribcage.

Internal retelling will shave the edges off eventually,
revealing the wisdom that was always underneath.

Rarely risk the open air.

The unspoken will often serve you better on the inside.

scorched earth

A wasteland of wreckage,
begins at the tip of your tongue.

Hold your fire.

Some fights can only be won,
if your goal in the beginning,
was to be alone in the end.

bridges

I've had my share of burnings.
But more often, neglect is what caused the collapse.
The letting go of the link,
in the hope of shaking any shame still attached.

Only to find it replaced by regret.

Others seem to live in a land of bridges.
Able to walk life's span,
without getting singed.
They accumulate associations,
and link one to the other effortlessly.

Then there are those of us who set controlled burns,
in order to manage connection without commitment.
Intending only temporary tie-up,
in our aversion to obligation,

Joining,
but then jumping.

In the end, it's the four-alarm losses that hold our biggest
lessons.
When we face the arsonist in the mirror every morning,
and long to rebuild what's been burned to the ground.

We've all wept over ashes at one time or another.

The bridges I build are much stronger these days.
After all, transient people still need to travel.
But I keep the spare parts from past incinerations to remind me.

I know what smoke smells like now.

messes

Be strong enough to manage the messes you make,
and brave enough to go make another.

There is no might before make,
and your crossed fingers hold no weight here.

Nothing changes,
if nothing happens,
and you're what happened last.

So, happen again,
and again,
and again.

Until the floor is covered in your consequences.

peace-ish

You wanted your peace to be pleasant,
like a picture.
You were even willing to repaint the past to make the present
match.
Desperate to simply be done,

or at the very least for a do-over.

But sometimes peace just means less war.
Sometimes it means predictable.
It almost never means perfect,

but it was always worth it to try.

cocoon

It's okay to want rain.
To wish for winter on the brightest day,
to long for dark rooms,
and thick blankets.

For night to come early.

There's nothing wrong,
with wanting rain,
when life is scorched,
and stinging the eyes.

The world wants us out there.
Summer months demand basking.
The rays send shame,
and light tugs at our legs.

All in good time.

Today is for the tucking in,
and licking of wounds.
The wallowing.

It's the perfect weather for it.

catch up

I used my old words for the longest time after.
Continued to tell my story,
as if it had always just happened.

Triggering the same system that got me stuck in the first place,
by letting my mouth lie to my life.

The vocabulary of your evolution is always expanding.
You were that once.
You're not anymore.
You've changed your life,

shouldn't you change how you describe it?

lightning

If you're lucky and life is long, you'll get the privilege of
grieving a great deal.
Transformative people will pass and take what you believe is
your very essence with them.
Your heart will swell to unimaginable sizes,
and will break into barely recognizable pieces.
Love will be responsible for all of it.

Admit that you've had time to measure,
and the cost is fair.
Life was never going to be only salt flats.
It's worth the deepest valleys for those amazing views.

You don't get to rig any future outcomes,
even as you build fortresses against your feelings.
Making bargains with unseen forces,
to promise only peaks if you agree to play again.

Half of the beauty was that you didn't see it coming in the first
place.

Lightning in a bottle may have been yours for a minute.
The broken glass that remains,
is the price of putting it in there in the first place.

doorways

You are free to go.
I have too much to do.

There are doorways everywhere.
They're counting on me.

The day is yours to design.
I said I would.

Was any of this your idea?
I can make do.

There is a reason you see doorways everywhere.
I don't see anything.

So much is waiting for your hand of creation.
It's only a hobby.

Life is vast and wide.
I'm out of time.

The future is limitless.
I'm lost.

There are doorways everywhere.
Please help.

You are free to go.

rock and a hard place

Much of life is determined by how you navigate the in-between.
Time spent in the space of having to choose.
Some take up residence for long stretches,
prolonging their suffering and pressing against the sides.
Others straddle and split themselves,
in their efforts to gain the benefit of 'both ways.'

But you already know what you have to do.
This is all just a holding cell before the sentencing.

Your character is carved in this crack.
Don't let delay become a destination.

Let granite grow within you.

lost in translation

You spent all of your words.
Believing if you emptied the tank,
a breakthrough would be found at the bottom.

I could have told you at the top.

What left your tongue,
transformed in the air,
and arrived in the shape of their story.

Their conclusions have no time for your corrections now.

Stop trying to make words do what only time can.

Let your life be your explanation.

This is a retraining worth working for.

silent treatment

'Tell me, what's wrong?' can be torture for some.

They know you can't bear to leave it unresolved.
That you're willing to shoulder unlimited blame for the
completely unknown,
if they would just stop holding 'we're okay' hostage.

Banished to the room inside yourself to think about what you've
done,
and sentenced to knocking on their shield,
as they dangle 'you know what you did' just out of reach.

This is where you've been trained to say you're sorry.
Followed by the fake relief of acting like it fixed anything,
but knowing it only feels better because it's familiar.

Getting 'giving in' down to a science.

But what if you left their silent treatment unsolved?
Simply took 'nothing' for an answer?
Committed to remaining rational,
and willing to talk,

but refusing to remain bullied.

And willing to wait through their wondering,
of why you're not scrambling to regain their favor.

This is a retraining worth working for.
A redirect of the trauma that's embedded on both sides,
that will feel far from good at first.

But if you stand firm in what's fair,
and hold compassion for the fact that their script feels carved in
stone too,

you might get a shot at an honest conversation,

as well as the feeling of a fair fight.

advice

It's better to endure the full force of their poison when you leave them,
than to have it delivered,
drop by drop,
for the

rest

of

your

life.

That's what I told her.

blinders

Be careful when dragging someone behind your agenda.
Always getting your way is not always a good thing.
They keep saying 'Sure, I guess',
so you go on believing you both made the choice.
Telling yourself, 'They're fine with it.'
Until one day they wake up and tell you they're living your life
and not their own.

And then they take your life with them when they leave.

storytime

For some, the story never ceases.
They wake to the retelling,
at times in mid sentence,
and run it like a fan in the background all day.

Forced to raise the volume of the surrounding thoughts,
in an effort to shout around it.

Silently adding new outrage to keep it fresh,
and calling in others to edit any new additions.

We've all been there at times.
Exhausting ourselves against the rocks of the repeating.
Determined to think the intolerable to death,
hoping another rerun will bring relief.

Or that this time our will can somehow bend the ending in our
favor.

This is simply a stage of grief we can't get around.

How we were hurt demands to be heard,
even if only on the inside.

look down

It's the challenge of childhood.
Trying to play the entire game,
with one foot on base.

Guarding.

Stretching yourself to your very limits.
Hoping to touch it all,
while risking nothing.
Checking the hue of the distant grass,
while remaining safe in your own yard.

You can play out most of a life this way,
and might already be doing so.

But where you're going means risking open air.
Surviving that moment between the release,
and the relief.

All while trusting yourself to bounce and begin again if you
have to.

Life comes down to a series of trust falls.

Keep learning to let go.

don't mind me

It's just the Placebo Effect.
Pay it no mind.
Dismiss your results.
A subconscious belief is only transforming and healing you.
A mere suggestion able to affect the physical.
You must immediately disregard.

There's nothing to point to that would prove that outcome,
therefore it didn't happen.
But it's charming you think so,
and I'm glad it gives you comfort.

We're going to be counting on you not to trust yourself,
with much higher stakes.
'All in your head' will mean wasteland,
not wonderland.

Seeds of self-doubt are the supplement.

Trust your gut,

but trust us more.

Seriously? 'Just' the Placebo Effect?

Mind over matter,
matters when it's your mind.

powerless

What we focus on expands.
That wound at your center,
has grown from an incident,
into an identity,
watered by all the attention.

We excavate our insides,
fill what's left with self-loathing,
then wonder where our worthiness went.

That which we don't want,
elevated to an art form.
A sculpture of our suffering.
Look what you made!

And you think yourself powerless?

It's the letting go of shame,
and the letting in of sunshine.

.

hero

Healing from any major surgery comes with an asterisk.
The body reminds in the form of sharp pain,
or aches when the weather changes.
Full movement may never return.

We accept this pain we can point to.

On and off physical therapy may be required,
simply to maintain, 'Not quite as broken'.
We lean into bad days,
understanding that doing nothing,
is exactly what our body needs.

It never gets labeled as lazy.

The body has been through a trauma,
and the endurance of lifetime healing,
takes immeasurable strength.

Hero stories start in this space.

Emotional trauma has its own punctuation.
The body is always along for the ride,
but the suffering is free flowing,
with a climate that's subject to change.

This kind of healing is given a deadline.

We deny this pain we can't point to.

We condemn ourselves for walking with an emotional limp,
and 'by now' is when we should be over it.

We suffer due to our definition.
We think 'healed' means residue free.
Placed back in the exact moment before IT happened,
the place where our old self lives.

We remember our full range of emotional motion,
and we want it back.

Erasing instead of incorporating.

But healing isn't dropping the load,
it's learning to shift the weight,
so the pain of carrying,
is shared among many.

It's the letting go of shame,
and the letting in of sunshine.

You are forever changed through trauma,
and the tools you gain in your recovery,
are needed for the rest of this trip.
Healing means not wanting to leave them behind.

Hero stories start here too.

sunflowers

It never occurred to me that sunflowers could grow wild.
I'd always held the belief they only grew in perfectly lined rows
of cultivated soil, waiting to be cut down, wrapped in plastic,
and placed for sale just inside the Trader Joe's entrance.
I imagine I thought they would be too fragile to thrive without
assistance and intervention,
but as I said,
I never imagined it at all.
Until they appeared on the trail that day.
A perfectly painted metaphor.
A field filled with '**pay attention**'
and suddenly a clearer picture of life emerged.

A life lived mostly in captivity.

We rarely get the chance to truly consider our containing.
Or our conditioning to need an abundance of assistance and
intervention in order to thrive.
'*Normal*' and '*expected*' need no further investigation,
it just never occurs to us.

And from the moment we bundle ourselves,
and give ourselves away for decoration,
our days are numbered.
But what's free in you will never stop trying to get your
attention,
reminding you that you were never just for display.

Stay feral enough to feel it.

armor

Check daily for the residue.
Remaining signs of emotional atrophy.
Dust for fading prints of bitterness,
and mark how far you've come.

You've earned this thicker skin,

but you're not required to carry it.

sliding doors

What happened at you,
to cause what happened in you?

Leave it untamed and untold,
and watch it grow over your path,
leaving you marked and unmarked,

depending on who's walking on you.

We pick at the edges of our identity,
to avoid excavation.
Re-masticating our memories,
in search of hidden flavors.

But you are more than a moment,
and your real life is under your origin story.
Your now being built on your then,
leaves a child in charge of the why.

Find the year,
and narrow from there.

Your expansion is now expected.

endurance

There is pain you must lean into alone.
Grief is rarely a group activity.
This is your proving ground,
even if you only lie on it.

Suffocated by all five stages at once.

Here is where you pay for how good it was.
For how much you were loved,
how much you lost,
and how it was worth every minute.

This is where your montage is made.

The unendurable demands your full attention.
Give it,
reside in it,
respect it,
and ultimately survive it.

Your growth is counting on you.

solo

I'm all alone.

And yet you're surrounded.

I don't fit in.

Because you're standing out.

I'm weary.

You're teaching us all endurance.

How much longer?

Truth has no timeline.

I'm all alone.

Not for long.

welcome home

The sign on the door reads:
'Here is where I rest in what's best for me, while leaving others free to manage their own feelings'.
A location that's probably taken you half a lifetime to locate.

Somewhere along the way, someone switched the sign to 'Selfish,'
so you learned to label it that way too.

Years of throwing yourself against the wall of outcome management and conversation orchestration have finally proven your powerlessness against those who would see you coming every time anyway,
and simply add another brick to it.

Even your ego has had to admit defeat,
and nothing has felt better since.

This is not the room of 'It's whatever, I don't even care.'
That's actually bitter's room trying to trick you again.
This is the place of compassionate indifference.
Caring without control.
Life's observation deck.
'What is' rules this place,
and acceptance does all the decorating.
Still can't tell if you're there?
The moment you start explaining yourself,
you're not anymore.

grace

Forgiveness can feel like nothing.
Euphoric absence,
with open hands,
and fresh blank pages.

It feels like everything else you now get to feel instead.

Like calm waters and personal accountability.

Like fewer reps.

It's in there,
living below all of the definitions.

Just something different now in the place where 'trying to' used
to live.

V

With creativity and the outdoors
getting a great deal of credit
for everything.

*To stand at the edge of yourself
and look down.*

my valentine

Admit that you're already in love.
That it may actually be the healthiest relationship of your life.
Confess to waking up and going to sleep with it in your thoughts.
Acknowledge that you're lost without it and miss it desperately when it tortures you with its absence.
That you often carry on this relationship in secret.

An artist is never really single.

We drop everything when it calls.
We start each day wondering how to increase the connection.
We create rituals designed to entice and adjust our approach when resistance is met.
Swinging from dominant to submissive willingly in its service.

Our passion makes us high.
Our feelings wind like vines through our work.
We wrap ourselves around our words and immerse ourselves in imagery.
What we are rewarded with defies explanation but does make a day on the calendar seem adorable, if not silly, in contrast.

If yours is a new relationship, then you're probably feeling pretty vulnerable right now.
That's normal and will never end.
You must be ready to be put in your place. A lot.
Each day will stretch you into new versions of yourself; some you will hate immensely.
Your ideas will often be rejected, but this is where trust comes in. You have to believe that your partner won't abandon you.

Get ready to feel abandoned at times.

But also prepare to feel that special kind of alive reserved for those who risk; to stand at the edge of yourself and look down. To gasp.
You will get a hint at the 'why' of it all.

As long as your 'how' is answered daily.

first aid

Creating is an exercise in walking backwards.
Not so much taking steps as retracing them.
Touring our own internal triage unit,
seeking wounds that can't wait any longer.
Or getting lost completely,
only to uncover new agonies by accident.

This is no coward's path,
but it is often a colorful one.
We're called to use our pain to paint for others,
and pretend it's only for something pretty to look at.

But we are healers.
Unafraid of the undiagnosed.

Especially in ourselves.

ripple

It's the ripple that we work for.
Our resonation.

Water moving, to show we mattered.

Will our words skip like rocks,
and echo when we're gone?
Or drop into the abyss,
seeking the silent bottom?

Fear of the latter keeps us glued to our craft.

Following breadcrumbs,
as if they are the last thing we'll ever eat.

For that which we will never see.

writer interrupted

A followed thought is a fragile thing.

We spend countless hours creating the calm,
that calls our chosen words forth.
Placing ideas like footsteps,
and testing the ground before continuing.
Checking behind and in front for connection.
As if letters could hold breath.

There is stillness in this battle.

The slightest tug from the surface,
means we have to start over.
Inching our way back in again.

Knowing we just lost a kingdom.

what god does | part 5

Then sometimes God closes a door,

and you like it better outside anyway.

thoreau

I went to the woods,
because I wished to live delightfully.
To stumble recklessly,
into realizing that the frivolous facts of life,
can fall within the category of essential too.
And that teaching comes in many forms,
and learning can be accidental.

It wasn't all said,
on the banks of Walden Pond,
by a man who wished to live before he died.
He left behind enough marrow for the rest of us,
and I intend to eat until I burst.

My account will forgo the meanness,
in favor of the magic.
And I don't so much want to drive it into a corner,
as I want to open up its skies.
I'll forgo its lowest terms,
in favor of its tallest trees.

As for my next excursion?
I'll bring you back my full account.
Enough to awaken your understanding,
that there's a little Thoreau in all of us,
and that your life,
and the woods,

are waiting.

born again

The edge of spring has its own special energy.
A collectively held breath.
For those of us who find our family in the woods,
this is our vigil.
Winter's labor, soon to be rewarded.

I can't wait to cry,
and water my view with awe.
Tears of gratitude at its rebirth,
reminding me yearly of my own.

For those of us who find our family in the woods,

we're expecting.

newborn

Everything is so swollen and lush right now.
Winter's runoff rushes through rivers and waterfalls.
Shades of green hold their own competition,
and new life presses to the front.
All in an effort to be born first.

I've had a few seasons to study this now,
while living through my own stark winters.
And though life has been frozen,
and all has been laid bare,
not once has nature stayed down.

The greatest beauty is always in the rebirth.
Life flashes and puts on a show.
We're paid back for our pain,
and new strengths are gifted,
'Fair' happens more and more often.

Be a student with every footstep.
Let what you find outside,
change how you live inside.

Your own winter's labor has made you ready.

Now push.

pnw

House Rules:
Arrive empty handed.
Don't overstay.
Your shoes are your own business,
but watch what you track.
Observe the two volumes,
of whisper or silence.
Help if you can.

Pray you get invited back.

Never forget whose house you're in.

We are made up of our detours.

rainier

Check for prints.
Tiny spiritual markings that say 'you alighted here.'
And here, now alights in you.
You are a crowded house of locations that tell your life story.

I am where my children were born.
You are where my life was saved.
He is where my dreams were lost.
They are where I found myself.

Entrances and exits provide life's punctuation.
Some are the commas of long pauses,
while others are simply dashes,
there to make one meaning from two.

The same you never lands twice.

I've been here as a woman,
and also a child.
A child's mother,
and a lost soul.
A day tripper,
and star gazer.
A storyteller,
and seeker.

Always acolyte,
and humble servant.

I am the multitudes on this mountain.

Here is where I've stood in awe,
and in grief.
I've felt as one,
and fully apart.

I have been humbled,
and I have felt holy.

Wholly.

We are made up of our detours
and destinations.
Our backwoods,
and upstairs bedrooms.
Our glass houses,
and thin ices.
Our bedrock,
and our blueprints.

We are mountains,
climbing mountains,
climbing mountains.

family trees

No one can tell you where to call home.
Out here, no one will.
You're worthy of your seat at each sunrise,
and the forest is indifferent to your birth order.

There is no branch for shame.

Peace grows wild,
and so do you.

Time and Earth will leave the porch light on.

VI

And part love letter.

what god does | part 6

Sometimes when you least expect it,

God just leaves the door open,

because you're worthy of things,

that won't fit through a window.

magic

'Tell me the story again from your side.'

We're like children when we're falling in love,
asking to once again hear how we got here.
Mining for clues of matched feelings.
Desperate to pin down the 'when did you know?'

I've been keeping this part of my story a secret,
'What if it doesn't work out?' ruling my words.
The illusion that no one knowing,
will somehow break me less.

I've guarded my growing trust like a newborn,
and see signs it will stand on its own.
So I'll be making room for him in my writing,

as they share the same heart now.

And if I'm ruined,
well, I would have written about it anyway,
So I don't want you to miss the good part.

falling

You didn't invent this.

The formula for falling lies deep within all of us,
as is the desire to lean back,
and let go.

But so is a healthy fear of heights.

Never relinquish the right to examine your life,
or the guest list.

Your blind side is still your business.

And while the colors may be dazzling,
two universes colliding,
can also change nothing.

Falling should not mean forgetting.

So scatter breadcrumbs in your wake,
you may need them to find your way back.

how love landed

'You only think you do,'
does its best to wedge its foot in after every 'I love you.'

Wiping it off the skin before it gets in,
and taking their word for it.

But then,
someone savors what you thought was unseen.
Proves they've been paying attention.
Drops in behind the line when your guards are changing shifts,
and the sudden belief takes your breath.

You will never be the same again.

But you weren't supposed to be.

hands

The clasp,

'Us'

learning thumb lines and nail shape.

Providing the push of encouragement,
or the pull in traffic.

Morse code,
'I'm here.'

Skin mined for guarantees,
of the never letting go.

A five-fingered trust fall from the greatest of heights.

I reach anyway.

Proof of how far I've come.

on being brave

I would have been happy to stay where I'd stopped growing.
Just getting there was my greatest masterpiece.
With 'healed' on display for all to see.
I had the exact right amount to manage.
And getting my way required nothing more of me than to give it
to myself.
Why chance what could end up in ruins?

Why risk rubble again?

I know that I will.
In fact, I already have.
But the conversation continues in my head daily anyway.

'Safe'
The one-word life goal that was lost when 'I no longer do'
happened,
and the reason I built the most beautiful bunker.
A party-of-one paradise filled with words and woods,
and extremely strict operating hours.

A nest padded with the proof of how far I've come.

And now we're painting what will be my office over at his place
this weekend.
Another step in our straddle.
Ever closer to the 'ours' that's currently under construction.
A stage of renewal,
that requires a partner to complete.

Fear will continue to stomp its feet and demand a say.
Afraid of what it will mean to let go of the old words,
in favor of ones that offer no guarantees.

And yet I will go.
And if I'm brave enough, I believe creativity will come with me,
and grant me new ways of weaving it all together.

Because we should be rewarded when we come out of hiding,
and prove we've recovered,

by taking it out on tour.

harvest

I walked around my growing trust today,
and marveled at the purity of its blooms.

How could this have come from the same ground where all my
broken parts are buried?

This thing I healed,
so I could now hold it for another.

Bouquets of believing in who I love.

two for one

I shouldn't complain about life getting crowded.
After all, I've handpicked the guest list,
and I fiercely guard the front door.

I'm simply trying to fit two lives,
into a model that barely provides for one.

The one that gets squeezed out,
is always the one they can't see.
It's hard to defend the 'doing nothing' that writing sometimes
looks like.

Creating can appear to be a quiet business.

My silent life is counting on me to provide the security.
To protect the one that provides light for the other.

Thank goodness I've found someone who loves both of us.

boundaries

Try this:

Fall into what feels like unlimited love.
Now, add some conditions.
Draw lines on the field so you both know what's 'out of bounds.'
Protect the perimeter you've had a lifetime to learn that you
need.

Risk the rejection of what you require.
Feel the fear of losing what you've placed in another,
but hold your boundaries with them anyway.

And watch yourself love two people at once.

first fight

I've been given the opportunity to resolve conflict while seeking
understanding and a deeper connection.

And I must politely decline.

My fresh wounds demand a cave and a closed door,
with all clarifying details locked safely on the other side.

The victim version of events must play out in a repeating cycle
of internal retelling,
and that isn't going to happen with the constant distraction of a
reasonable explanation.

There will be time for less delusion later.

For cooler air to soothe our sentences,
and for being on the same side,
to remind us of it.

But not yet.
The lockdown has already been loaded,
and this is the side of the story I'm sticking to.

Sometimes being wrong needs to wait.

broken glass

It happened again.

Someone's fresh new words,
traveled through my broken filter,
and set up camp with my embedded fears.
The name they came up with was 'True.'
Favorite activity: Cliff diving.

Where we've been has no choice but to act as the translator for
where we're going.
Unfortunately, it only speaks,
'Here we go again.'

We spent two hours untangling.
Re-walking each word,
back to its original meaning.

The one where we love each other.

Comparing cracked lenses.
Finding the moment that fear faked us out.
Adjusting our focus.
Seeing each other without the story.

Making us grateful for a little broken glass.

blending

We're taking what is currently under construction out for its first full test drive this weekend.

Two tight-knit groups of three,
taking on a bigger dinner table.

Broken families,
with well-matched edges.

The children we lead are much larger now,
but he and I know they still look to us,
to look out for them.
And to know that each is holding their own quiet question:

How do I fit here?

Our job is to give them enough room to find their own answers,
and the assurance that new changes won't touch the things that
never will.

By this time next week something new will have happened.
A group formed,
as the result of one gathering,
and a table full of seats will be set in stone.

The coming years will bring messes and miracles in equal
measure,
with love and acceptance threaded through each.

It will be beautiful,
but it will never be perfect.

Thank God,

because no family ever is.

*The outcome, somehow installed
like a new appendage.*

family meeting

An accidental opportunity on a Saturday,
brought most of the future roles together in front of the fireplace.
Something true was said,
a small split in a scar,
and authentic thoughts poured out through the opening.
Secret apprehensions hidden behind the happiest of upcoming
occasions.
The family we're making,
flexing its fears for the first time.

Worried that this new life will erase that which we aren't ready
to lose.

A trust-fall conversation.
Unplanned,
yet everyone's arms were out.

Silent bargains were made in return for the right words.
Each one placed with so much care.
Checking in front and behind for fit,
before letting another one land on the foundation of 'How you
feel matters.'

So much was riding on the weather in that room.
But every person in it had already fought personal storms far
greater than the difficulty of a deep conversation,
so wounded words never once met resistance.
And no one's defenses demanded a say.

I woke up in the morning,
wrung out in the right way.
Verbally bone tired,
with the memory of weighted words,
and new emotional muscle.
The outcome, somehow installed like a new appendage.

The body, recording a big conversation.

We will stand and say words next month, he and I,
with our children at our wings.
A ceremony that may only last a few minutes.
A wedding party gathered by the fire in candlelight.

But last weekend,
in front of that exact same fireplace,
I got a lot more married.

The story I'll be telling will be about a time of healing and growth, with lessons so lush, I might have stayed there learning forever.

love letter to the last seven years

Sometimes we get to circle an entire section of time,
and place a giant X at the center.

'Here will be the hardest years of your life. Use them wisely.'

It all started with a math problem:
One year of recovery for every five years I had been married.
A sentence demanding to be served before real life would be
resumed.

A time chasm.

With no guarantees of how it would all turn out.

Would fetal remain my favorite position?
Would angry and bitter eat me alive?
Would I dodge my own accountability in favor of the victim
version of events?
Was I destined to only use the time to tell the story?

I'm aware that this all sounds a lot like years one and two,
but in my defense, fear still had me by the throat back then.
I'd still live through them again if I had to though,
if only for the trees and trails.

I'll be saying words next week,
that will make the work we've done here worth every minute,
but I'll still be grieving that you're gone.

And the story I'll be telling will be about a time of healing and
growth,
with lessons so lush,
I might have stayed there learning forever,
if it weren't for the rest of my years waiting for their turn.

But I couldn't just leave without saying goodbye.
Or without letting you know something important happened here,
and everything I'll be next,
is better because of it.

I hope I made you proud.

the day

My left leg seemed to have its own Richter scale,
most of it hidden by the dress.
Centering breath.
Nothing written down.

Songbird
Stairs
Faces

'*I'll start with I love you*' is how I began.
The rest, now lost to the blur.
We anchored our eyes and let our words work out the details.
Knitting.

Candles
Tears
Rings

Kiss

Flanked by our children,
each with a toast that brought tears.

Love
Grief
Growth
Laughter

In case there was still any doubt about the job we've done.

Peach spoke of La Push and its place in our story.
'When she took you there, I knew.'

Woods
Water
Healing
Holy

So did I.

From after and alone you asked, 'How does it feel?'
'The same,' was my answer.

Sure
Worthy
Right
Honored

Loved

Exactly the same.

committed

I say 'my husband' now when talking about him to others.

Marveling at how the words can feel at once so foreign, and yet so familiar.

Learning the language of the rest of my lifetime.

This is a good thing.

'Can I be with you and still be me?' was a question I began asking him early, and often.

He never once lost patience when he answered.

And yet,

I would worry anyway.

Anyone who knows how change works would.

Will I slowly forget the girl in the woods, and only see her on somedays?

Will 'shoulds' keep me away from the shores?

Will I forget where the air is made, and return to breathing in the top two inches in my life?

Will my wild give way to, 'I don't care, what do you want?'

Will I go back to sleep in myself?

But then I come to a curve in the road, with the wall of the world painted in trees and hilltops.

Life layered in front of me as far as I can see.

Telling me 'There's water this way', and a moment's notice is all I need.

And I am filled with the kind of belonging that can only happen when you're alone.

And I think to myself,

'There she is.'

That girl isn't going anywhere.

VII

Epilogue

All of the me's will gather one day,

On a stage filled with all of my lives.

Each hoping for the highest honor,

Wanting to know,

Who came closest?

The me from my childhood will push to go first,

Claiming the foundation years as the purest.

Citing her humor and imagination,

Taking credit for the woods and the water.

She will make a powerful case.

The 'hoping to be loved' of my teen years will have everyone's compassion,

Simply because she had the job of building the armor,

And didn't mean to overdo it.

The one who couldn't stop without help will sit stripped to the bone in the back,

Holding coffee and waiting her turn to talk.

By the way, once she does, you may believe we need look no further.

The 'I do' version was me for the longest,

And still tells the story too much,

But the one who became the 'I'm here' for two others,

Knows her position is safe.

Each era will vie for top honors,

And there will be debate over when one became the other.

They won't get any closer,

That was never really the point.

I was always the one who invited them.

And who I'll be next has already started.

VIII

Just one more thing...

acknowledgements

Please don't go just yet.

I promise to try and make the reading of this part worth it.

I'll spin a wonderful poem that I will eventually name 'Acknowledgements.'

It will include all of the elements of great storytelling to go along with the gratitude.

There will be heroes, epiphanies, spiritual experiences and the great outdoors. Along with some delightful coincidences.

There will even be a love interest!

As well as the promise of 'ever after' being just over that ridge.

So let's begin:

Once upon a time,

or roughly three or so years ago,

I was sitting on my bed, contemplating regrets I would have if I were to die, when I had a spiritual experience.

As anyone who's ever had one knows, trying to describe it can often only take you further away from the actual feeling,

but I'll do my best.

My fleeting thought was, 'I would probably regret never really exploring my writing.'

At that moment, I had a very clear awareness of a response.

An understanding,

and an offering.

The closest I can come to an example, is that when I was a kid, and I was interested in something that cost money, my dad would always say, 'I'll meet you halfway,' as a way to communicate that if I was willing to put in the effort, that he would supply the rest.

On this night, there were no words exchanged, but the sense of 'I'll meet you halfway,'

flooded me.

So, I must say thank you to the 'All' that I don't yet fully understand.

This partnership has been one of the most rewarding relationships of my life. Your daily contributions have woven their way through my writing.

And while my name goes on the book, we both know that 'writer' isn't something I do alone.

I began my 'daily column' the next day.

Joking to my loved ones about being on a 'deadline.'

Pretending it wasn't all that serious, just something to do during quarantine.

I knew I had dedication, but I lacked any kind of direction.

(The princess enters during this part. We'll call her Peach.)

On the fourth day, Peach suggested I start a blog so I would have a place to share my work.

(Now, dear reader, I am in danger of potentially making this a second book if I try and tell the entire story, so please forgive my need to jump to the point.)

To my incredible daughter Peach,

there has been so much magic attached to this journey, and it seems that you are its favorite element to work with.

Thank you for the hours spent teaching me how to navigate the online world.

Thank you for taking all of this seriously long before I was ready to say out loud that I did too.

Thank you for that 'dark days' text asking me to run away to the coast, and thank you for driving on every single trip that followed.

You are the only other person I can be 'alone' in the woods with.

Thank you, also, for putting your fingerprints on every single page of this book.

You took a series of snapshots and created a beautiful story.

I'm so grateful I gave birth to the initiator of my life's biggest left turn.

Now, I can't speak of my blog without addressing all of the people I believed would never read it. So, to every person who ever read or shared my work, who messaged me with encouragement, who said, 'I can't wait to read your book one day.'

Thank you for being such an amazing community. Our daily conversations have been the most wonderful and unexpected surprise. Without your frequent declarations of 'I feel that way too!'

I might have lost my momentum. I look forward to many more years discovering together.

Okay, we've come to the dashing knight part!

A dashing knight with a discerning eye for poetry and literature entered the scene during my Act Two, and we fell in love for completely unrelated reasons.

He accepted my strange writing hours, but I was initially shy about sharing much, worried that he would think it was only a cute 'hobby', or even worse, that he wouldn't like it. I won't dwell on those things, because they didn't happen.

What happened instead is the kind of belief, support and encouragement that can make things transform into solid form.

The kind that becomes contagious.

To Ric. This book became a reality because of you. Thank you for knowing for both of us for a while, and for reminding me repeatedly.

Loving and trusting you in all things has become one of my new favorite activities.

I look forward to the rest of a lifetime of it.

So now we had the idea firmly in place, all we needed were the magic words, which just happened to come tumbling out on a walk one day:

'I just need someone to tell me what to do. Step by step. Start to finish.'

Once they were spoken, I realized that person had been placed in my path all the way back at the beginning.

Thank you Jill Carlyle, and The Empowered Press.

I truly believe we were meant to work together to bring this book to life, and I've been massively rewarded for figuring out the obvious.

I had finally gotten the courage to say 'I'm a writer,'

but you made me an author.

Step by step.

Start to finish.

By telling me what to do.

Thank you for breaking this process down into bite sized pieces that even a creative mess like me could manage.

So this is it.

We've come to the end of why I asked you to stay.

And I'm glad I'm no longer the only one who knows about the shoulders planted firmly under my feet.

But I can't just thank all of the players, and not mention how critically important the setting has been.

And so,

to First Beach in La Push.

To the Cape Disappointment Lighthouse,

and Highway 101,

to Second Beach,

and Third.

To Rialto and Ruby beaches.

To Cape Flattery,

and Seiku.

To the Hoh Rain Forest,

and the Olympic National Forest.

To each and every San Juan Island,

and the Washington State Ferry System.

To Mount Rainier,

and Snoqualmie pass.

To every tiny 'positioning' hotel up the Oregon and Washington coasts.

To Forks and the Twilight Motor Inn.

To 'My Trail' that I walked so often, if it hadn't been there before then my footsteps would have blazed it.

And finally, to each and every evergreen tree in the Pacific Northwest.

I had no idea when I started what a significant part you would play.

Thank you for being the symbol for my insides.

And in case I missed anywhere:

To every square inch of this beautiful Pacific Northwest.

I saw every single sign that you sent me.

And I will never make another major life decision without checking with you first.

- Lainey